For Karen Scawen

**Many thanks to the staff and children at
Discovery Montessori Day Nursery and
Teeny Tots Nursery for their help and advice.**

Copyright © 1996 De Agostini Editions Ltd
Illustrations copyright © 1996 Paul Hess

Edited by Anna McQuinn, designed by Sarah Godwin

While every effort has been made to trace the present copyright holders
we apologize in advance for any unintentional omission or error and will
be pleased to insert the appropriate acknowledgment in any subsequent edition.
Grateful acknowledgment is made to the following for permission to reprint the material listed below:
The Cow copyright © 1983 by Jack Prelutsky from **Zoo Doings**, reprinted by permission
of Greenwillow Books (a division of William Morrow & Company, Inc).
Cock a doodle doo, **Pig Shaving** and **Goosey Gander** are the classic versions
collected by Peter and Iona Opie from **The Oxford Nursery Rhyme Book**, 1955,
reprinted by permission of Oxford University Press.
The Sheep by Ann Taylor and **My Doggie** by C. Nurton from **The Book of a Thousand Poems** copyright © 1983
Bell & Hyman Limited, first published in 1942 by Evans Brothers Limited, reprinted by permission of HarperCollins.
Goat copyright © 1994 Miles Gibson. Reprinted by kind permission of Jonathan Clowes Ltd., London, on behalf of Miles Gibson.

First published in the United States by De Agostini Editions Ltd, 919 Third Avenue, New York, NY 10022
Distributed by Stewart, Tabori & Chang, a division of U.S. Media Holdings, Inc., New York, NY

ISBN 1-899883-34-7
Library of Congress Catalog Card Number: 96-83066

Printed and bound in Italy

Farmyard
Animals

Illustrated by
PAUL HESS

Sheep

LAZY SHEEP, pray tell me why
In the grassy fields you lie,
Eating grass and daisies white,
From the morning to the night?

Rooster

COCK A DOODLE DOO!
My dame has lost her shoe,
My master's lost his fiddling stick
And knows not what to do.

Cow

THE COW mainly moos as she chooses to moo...
and she chooses to chew as she muses.

Horse

HORSEY, HORSEY don't you stop!
Just let your feet go clippety-clop.
Tail goes swish and wheels go round.
Giddy Up! We're homeward bound!

Goat

THE GOAT – a sort of sheep with horns
Must live on thistles, roots and thorns
Which might explain his fractious bouts
Of chasing brownies and boy scouts.

Pig

BARBER, BARBER, shave a pig,
How many hairs will make a wig?
Four and twenty, that's enough.
Give the barber a pinch of snuff.

Goose

CACKLE, CACKLE, Mother Goose,
Have you any feathers loose?
Truly have I, pretty fellow,
Half enough to fill a pillow.

Dog

I HAVE A DOG, his name is Jack.
His coat is white, with spots of black.
Such clever tricks, my dog can do,
I love my Jack, he loves me too!